Wheels

Words by Madden Hay
Pictures by Alan Benge

One wheel.

Two wheels.

Three wheels.

Four.

If the wheels
fall off,

Try once more.

Big wheels and small.

No wheels at all.

Fast wheels.

Slow wheels.

Best of all,

My wheels,

My bike,

My bicycle.

Independent reader checklist:

☑ Repetition of vocabulary aids reading and spelling.

☑ Key topic words aid comprehension.

☑ Rhythm and rhyme help with pronunciation and enjoyment.

☑ Reading-friendly font helps all readers especially those with dyslexia.

☑ Pictorial cues help with guessing unknown vocabulary.

Copyright © Madden Hay 2025

ISBN 978-1-0670286-6-4
Text by Madden Hay
Pictures by Alan Benge
Tyre pattern by Freepik

First published by Piwaiwaka Press
www.piwaiwakapress.com
163 Rata Street, Naenae
Lower Hutt 5011
New Zealand

All rights reserved. This book is copyright. Except for the purposes of fair review, no part of this book may be stored or transmitted or reproduced in any form or by any means, electronic or mechanical, including recording or storage in any information retrieval system, without permission in writing from the publisher. Madden Hay asserts their right to be known as the author of this work.

www.ingramcontent.com/pod-product-compliance
Lightning Source LLC
Chambersburg PA
CBHW042053030526
44119CB00061B/493